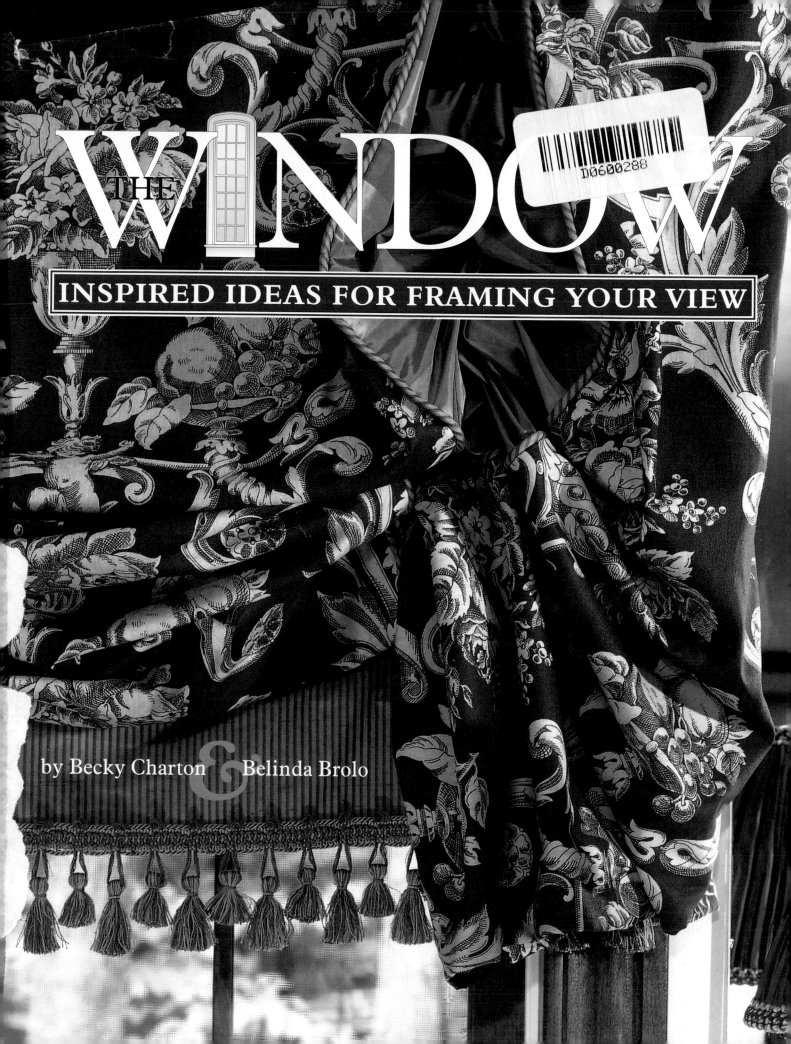

# THE WINDOW

## INSPIRED IDEAS FOR FRAMING YOUR VIEW

by Becky Charton & Belinda Brolo

# THE W█NDOW

**EDITORIAL STAFF**
Vice President and Editor-in-Chief: Sandra Graham Case
Executive Director of Publications: Cheryl Nodine
 Gunnells
Director of Designer Relations: Debra Nettles
Editorial Director: Susan Frantz Wiles
Publications Director: Susan White Sullivan
Art Operations Director: Jeff Curtis

**EDITORIAL AND TECHNICAL**
Technical Managing Editor: Mary Sullivan Hutcheson
Editor: Sherry T. O'Connor

**ART**
Art Publications Director: Rhonda Shelby
Art Imaging Director: Mark Hawkins
Art Category Manager: Lora Puls
Designer/Graphic Artist: Dale Rowett
Imaging Technicians: Stephanie Johnson and Mark Potter
Staff Photographer: Russell Ganser
Publishing Systems Administrator: Becky Riddle
Publishing Systems Assistants: Clint Hanson, Myra
 Means and Chris Wertenberger

**BUSINESS STAFF**
Publisher: Rick Barton
Vice President, Finance: Tom Siebenmorgen
Director of Corporate Planning and Development:
 Laticia Mull Cornett
Vice President, Retail Marketing: Bob Humphrey
Vice President, Sales: Ray Shelgosh
Vice President, National Accounts: Pam Stebbins
Director of Sales and Services: Margaret Reinold
Vice President, Operations: Jim Dittrich
Comptroller, Operations: Rob Thieme
Retail Customer Service Managers: Sharon Hall and
 Stan Raynor
Print Production Manager: Fred F. Pruss
Director of Public Relations and Retail Marketing:
 Stephen Wilson

Made in the United States of America.

Library of Congress Catalog Number 2002116553

International Standard Book Number 1-57486-314-2

10 9 8 7 6 5 4 3 2 1

CON

*Each and every day, life brings the unexpected. Some surprises are large and some are small. The day the idea for this book was born was one of those "big surprise" days.*

**Becky**: I was standing on a ladder accessorizing a kitchen when I was asked if I would be interested in producing a book on window treatments. "Of course," I said. "Let me come down from the ladder."

**Belinda**: I was at home working on a project and the phone rang. It was Becky with an invitation—not only to lunch, but to join together to produce a long-time dream of mine.

*Creating this book has given us both the opportunity to do what we enjoy doing best, sharing great ideas. When we look back, we realize our destinies were decided long before business cards, logos, and portfolios were chosen.*

**Becky**: When I look back, I'm amazed to realize it's completely natural to do what I do today. From the time I was a small child, I loved order, coordinating, and style. I loved to organize my grandmother's Avon closet, set her tables for Sunday dinner, and rearrange the accessories in the pink bedroom with the pink chenille bed cover. I remember in third grade building a desk out of boxes in my closet. I liked the fact that I could close the door and have a clean look. In ninth grade, my mother finally allowed me to have my own Christmas tree filled with starched lace fans, plaid ribbon, and white lights in the formal living room. When I was first married, I thought it was a fun hobby to help all my friends set up house—organizing kitchens, hanging pictures, and arranging furniture. After nine years of working in a creative career unrelated to interior design, I "retired" to begin my own business, *Table Setters*, which allowed me, then and now, the outlet for my love and my hobby.

I remember sharing with my husband Kevin how I felt about my new venture. "When I leave a home, I want my client to have ownership, I want them to call the project 'theirs', not their decorator's." I often think all my careers have really been facets of just one, the career of giving.

I am so grateful for the handful of people who mentored me, giving away their values, creativity, and work ethic: my grandparents, Mother and Father, and some special friends and teachers—Martha, who had a locked gift closet full of wrapped gifts ready to give; Lynn, a true lady who wore design on the outside and exuded beauty from within; Mrs. Freeburg, my second-grade teacher who gave me a "most creative" award; and Mrs. Ayers, my high-school drama teacher who welcomed dressing up just to read prose.

We all have an opportunity to give away our gifts and talents, some by pure observation, others by allowing people into our homes and lives. Thank you to all who allowed me to create within myself and within your homes.

**Belinda:** I was probably five years old when I first wanted a sewing machine. My friend Teri had a toy one, and we would spend hours trying to make it work. Well, I was thirteen when my mother bought me my first real sewing machine. Soon I was actually creating all the clothes I had sketched and colored in Mrs. Hearn's class. I didn't know then that this would be the machine that would launch a cottage business called *Tea Time*, where I made hand-smocked tea-length dresses. Eventually, because of the workload, I entered the computer age, purchasing a new machine that would not only make my tea-time dresses more efficiently, but also more timely.

Years later, that second machine became the workhorse for another venture, *Curtain Call, Inc.*, my drapery design business that I run today. In another life, I would have loved to play Chrissy for the Wimbledon title, as tennis was my second passion, but my love for home and finding ways to make it beautiful became, and still is, my center court.

Mrs. Virginia, who made my skating outfits, and my Aunt Betty, a master seamstress who always sent my sister and me boxes of beautifully designed clothes, are responsible for sparking my curiosity about the process of design. Having a mother who was and is an encourager and a father who was my greatest teacher and mentor provided the foundation and the freedom to be … me.

*With this book, our wish is that you receive what we've given you—then dream, create, and exercise the freedom to be… you!*

—*Becky Charton and Belinda Brolo*

Looking Out,

*A friend once told us, "There are two things a home can never have too many of...trees and windows." We all know the many advantages majestic trees offer the outdoor spaces they so gracefully embrace—privacy, shade, security, structure, and most of all beauty. Windows offer many of these same amenities for the indoor spaces that make up our homes.*

*All windows, though, are not created equally. What do the windows in your home offer? Do they reveal a perfect view that you'd never wish to cover up, or do they allow you to look a little too closely onto an unsightly view? What parts of your window would you like to emphasize—the lovely lines of an arch or intricate moldings that frame a view? What parts would you like to hide—the heat and glare of the evening sun, or is the entire window simply the wrong size for a room?*

*In this book, you'll meet some wonderful people whose homes hold some of our favorite window treatments. We'll show you how we enhanced windows that were already gorgeous and how we transformed problem windows into assets. Together we'll take a tour of design ideas, fabrics, hardware, and the accessories that make a window special. Plus, we'll share some cost-cutting strategies you're sure to love. Most of all, we hope this book will inspire you to take a serious look at your home's windows and give you a fresh perspective on designing treatments that best suit the needs of yourself and your family.*

Looking In

# Creating Designs

*When designing a suitable window treatment,
consider function, lighting, privacy, view, and – of course – beauty.*

## To Function or Not to Function

Stationary window dressings are appropriate
for rooms where we simply want to enhance
beauty, soften hard lines, convey warmth,
or create a focal point. They are motionless
but their presence frames and completes
their surroundings.

## Too Much of a Good Thing…Light

We must harness light and control it, for if
we allow it to dominate it will fade,
deteriorate, and even over time rot the fabrics
and artwork in our spaces. West-facing
windows, especially, may need treatments
that can control the heat and damaging rays.
Insulating by means of using thermal lining,
in addition to interlining or even blackout
lining, helps to reduce the harmful effects
of a good thing.

## Privacy, Please

There are of course, those days that scream
out at us, where noise, objects, and people
clutter and overwhelm our innermost beings.
At the end of a hectic day, we long for
seclusion. Our window treatments can provide
sanctuary in many functional ways, such as:
a simple stationary sheer, a lowered roman
shade, a pulled silk panel, the draw of a
bamboo shade, or, if luxury permits, a push
of a button that will automatically give you
tranquility. In the privacy of our own homes,
we find refuge.

## Inside or Out

Do we frame the window for the beauty that
exists on the inside or coax the beauty of the
outdoors in? If our outdoor view is that of a
neighbor's unkempt yard, our window needs
to promote beauty from within. However,
should our outlook be cascading perennials
around a lush pond with lotus blooms the
color of sunshine, our treatment of choice
should only complement the outside image.

## Beauty or the Beast

Today's new homes are being trimmed
out, landscaped, customized, and offered
up to a more sophisticated and savvier buyer.
Windows in these homes seem to be larger
than life. Beautiful moldings adorn
translucent pieces of glass, just as gilded
frames surround the works of Van Gogh and
Renoir. For windows that are "molded to the
extreme," plantation shutters or wide
wooden blinds may be all that's needed.
But there are always creative ways to
enhance even a beautiful window.

Worst-case window scenario? You have a
beautiful room with a beast of a window—
out of proportion, too small for the scale of
the room, or simply misplaced. These
windows challenge the best in us. This is
where we really must be creative and
approach the task in an artistic fashion.
Think of the window as if you are simply
placing one more complementary accessory
to complete your gorgeous space.

The Dentons' renovated ranch-style home demonstrates a perfect example of *scale*, as large, expansive rooms offer abundant space for entertaining, family gatherings, New Year's parties, or hosting the neighborhood Bunco group. This home also has one more amenity to offer than most: an in-house decorator. So, when approaching the window options, decisions were expedited accordingly. The living room's elongated picture window needed balancing. To magnify the height, but at the same time shorten the width of the window, the rod was placed at the ceiling line. Large buffalo plaid silk panels dropped from gold rings added weight. To further break up the horizontal lines of the window, we inserted overlapping swags to give movement. Sometimes a balancing act is required when approaching certain projects.

scale

S ecluded on the point of a lake, this home sits but a stone's throw away from water's edge. Beauty and serenity are ever present, even when we reach the couple's bedroom. Awestruck are our senses when we step into this master suite where the homeowners' love of *beauty, scale, and balance* are amply demonstrated. Two sets of triple arched windows surrounded by ornate moldings frame the view of the lake. To accent the lines of the windows, but take nothing away from the moldings, a cornice was constructed to simply follow the lines as if molding and cornice were one entity. The fabric colors— aubergine and nectarine—are a designer's dream. Take special notice of the banding on the panels as your eyes move across the page. There is so much offered here, so much to grasp, why not pour another cup of tea and dream a little longer.

*&balance*

A stone bungalow in the heart of a historical neighborhood was the perfect placement for this **French Country** valance. Featherlike poppies and woven gingham make for a flawless beginning to a picture-perfect end. Our goal was to play off the crown molding and allow it to not only frame the window, but also frame the valance. The ornate crown that frames this 1928 window had shifted a little on one side over the years. To correct this slight problem, we simply raised one bracket a little higher than the other. The wispy swags with the pleated ruffle whisper softly, "Ooh-la-la."

*french country*

The window above is layered with amazing moldings. To continue the theme, layers of draperies were applied, thus solidifying a very pronounced design statement. For the room's integrity, the silk offers **richness**. The swags' soft motions remove the hard lines of the molding, while the cascades and jabots trimmed with six-inch bullion fringe add a degree of wonderful decadence.

# elegance

**A**s you approach the double doors to this elegant home, you bask in the formality, but you're not intimidated. Passing through the doors, marble encircles your feet. You're impressed, but still not intimidated. Beautiful furnishings arranged for perfect conversations, silks muffling the sounds of children playing and dogs barking—it's a beautiful home for a growing family. There's lots of living space, but a portion is reserved for more refined gatherings. Silk swags offer the repetition needed to convey *elegance*. From marble floors to understated ceiling, from accessories to furnishings, balance is everything.

17

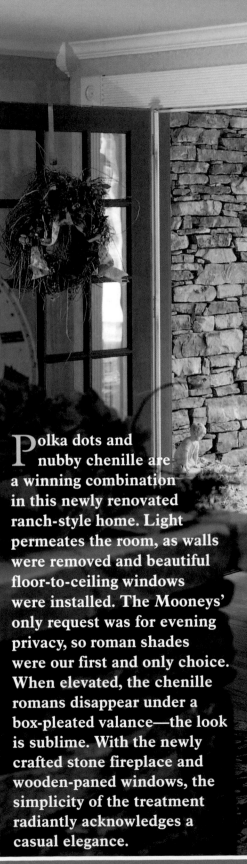

*impact*

T he sunken family room with its vaulted ceiling gave this room marvelous height to work with our window design. The only challenge was that the paneled room had only one corner window, so light became a concern. We had one small window to make a huge *impact*. This was accomplished by the design of an oversized cornice hung at the ceiling line. Sissy relayed her need for light and privacy, so a soft stationary sheer was placed inside a pair of traversing silk drapes.

P olka dots and nubby chenille are a winning combination in this newly renovated ranch-style home. Light permeates the room, as walls were removed and beautiful floor-to-ceiling windows were installed. The Mooneys' only request was for evening privacy, so roman shades were our first and only choice. When elevated, the chenille romans disappear under a box-pleated valance—the look is sublime. With the newly crafted stone fireplace and wooden-paned windows, the simplicity of the treatment radiantly acknowledges a casual elegance.

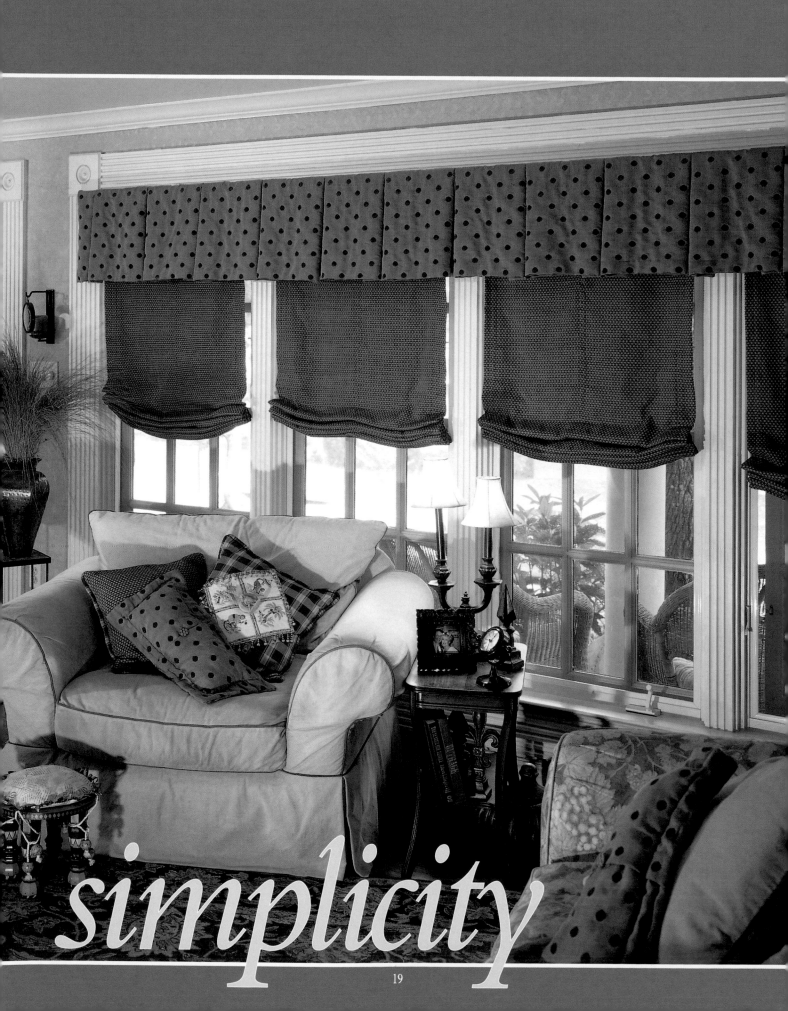

*simplicity*

This client's bedroom perches on the eighth hole of a golf course, where only a dozen or so pine trees obscure fourteen feet of windows. Lighting was sufficient; her only need was privacy. So, with twenty-plus yards of black dupioni silk fabric and a pull of a baton, her bedroom becomes her *private domain*. A black and taupe stripe accentuates while adding dimension to the large amounts of yardage needed to cover this grand expanse. Careful measurements were taken to insure the stack back would slide sufficiently past the window. Looking out her window, she may just envision a hole in one.

*private domain*

F ourteen-foot ceilings give this modern home *(above)* a *lofty view* of the golf course. Symmetry, harmony, and balance imply perfect form for the golfer and the breakfast room. Panels were hung at the ceiling to give full appreciation for the height of the room. Lined and interlined, the treatments absorb mealtime chatter and are sometimes even the center of lively discussion.

It's always nice when a home has a *formal* entry *(left)*, offering a proper introduction to the personality of the home. Doors that include sidelights allow light to filter in, but may require a treatment for privacy. These tiny roman shades present a solution for seclusion and the bonus of a design element. Remember when using fabrics with stripes, those stripes must line up perfectly.

*formal*

Can you fathom moving
42 times in 47 years, existing
as a military brat for 16 years,
serving in the U. S. Navy for
six years, traveling from the
Ishikawa Beach off the coast
of Okinawa, Japan, to the exotic
and beautiful Palma de Majorca
in the Mediterranean? The
unique man who has practically
lived a travelogue deserves to be
pampered when he comes home.
For Marco, we felt that his love
of beauty should permeate his
home, especially since this is his
first permanent home. The
*dramatic* window in this master's
master suite is most certainly a
focal point. Forty-four yards of
silk complete the room fit for a
king. A design faux pas that some
might make is to cut the window
in half by placing the rod right
under the arch. We chose to
place the rod at the very top.
The eyes then follow the regal
drape of fabric that accents the
room's generous molding and
deep tray ceiling.

*dramatic*

23

# Selecting Fabrics

**The selection of fabrics is the second most important element in your window treatment design.**

*When we speak of the very fabric of our nation, are we speaking of denim? We think not. But show us a person on whom a pair has not graced her derrière! Well, the choices for window coverings far exceed good ol' denim, and thank goodness. Our favorite fabric, silk, has made its way well into the mainstream of American décor, but a host of other fabulous textiles are out there:*

Rich Chenilles     Translucent Sheers
Woven Damasks     Crisp Taffetas
Raw Linens     Pictorial Toiles
Blended Polyesters     Supple Velvets
Graceful Rayons     Traditional Wools

*Let's not forget to mention the embellishments rendered onto the above list of yardages. There are embroidered and manipulated silks, colorful toiles de Jouy not limited to pastoral scenes, and mirrored cottons. What about hand-painted silks, crinkled rayons, beaded polyesters, and acid-washed velvets? Then, there are pocketed, embroidered, and stamped sheers and a host of other artistic applications. We suggest you venture out and discover the multitude of choices that await you. Fabric selection is important, but most of all, it's fun!*

ORIGIN

Approaching the walkway that leads to this historic 1929 Spanish Mediterranean villa, you can't help but be seduced by the beautiful arched window that beckons you inside. Almost as if impersonating an omniscient eye, it follows and assists your movements from the front path to the heavily studded copper door. Once inside, you can appreciate the treatments adorning this coaxing window and the windows flanking an original stucco fireplace. The main drapery *(left)* is composed of six different fabrics and textures, a lesson in variety. Its origin and use of textiles is Moroccan, each layer complementing the next. Self-cording, embroidered tape, and ball fringe are more than sufficient to complete the ***originality*** of this imposing window. Softly shirred balloon shades *(above)* on the other windows offer a vivid yet constrained repeat of the stripe motif.

A L I T Y

**H**and-smocked dresses and French braids in her hair are all but memories now that Jordan is all grown up. When she returns home for visits she darts in and dashes out. As parents, Marco and I just feed her and give her money. And, of course, we like for her to get a good night's sleep after all that darting and dashing. The window in her home-away-from-home was designed for sleeping late. At her age, fun and funky is what it's all about. Ribbed cotton, apple green check, ball fringe and Indian cotton are awfully energetic. The Indian cotton center panel allows filtered light to shadow the room, while the two side ribbed panels can be pulled for privacy and *"sleeping inn."*

28

# PIZZAZZ

**D**esigns need not be intense or difficult to offer *pizzazz*. Take for instance these simple triangles. The sharp angles make a perfect play for the plaid and animal skin print to hit a home run. The entrance to this home allows us to view multiple rooms. Selecting fabrics for all the rooms was made easy by using parallel palettes of spicy colors.

*elegant*

Just off the living room sits this intensely *elegant* dining room *(above)*. Soft gathers of the balloon romans add just the right romantic touch. The history of toile adds a traditional ambiance, but the choice of a silk toile only affirms elegance. When the shade is raised a plaid silk lining lends an element of surprise. The third and final layer is a wonderful silk stripe accented with a beautiful tassel trim. Study the layering of the fabrications closely on this design, then pull down the shades and enjoy dinner.

Carpools, baseball games, practices, school volunteering ... With many days filled with all of the above, it's a wonder a mom finds time to find herself. For the years spent raising our young children, we seem to lose part of our selves in the process. Each evening at bedtime, though, as we relinquish our duties for the day, we can *retreat* once again into our private worlds. Well, at least sometimes. For Trish, her bedroom windows *(right)* allow her to escape to the serenity of the pool. Sheer panels bursting with color and an Asian motif add intrigue and interest and hopefully help her to absorb the day's activities.

retreat

We admit it: we've gone monkey crazy! Those trend-setting little creatures are everywhere! When a hot idea hits the decorating scene, you're sure to find it translated into just about everything. No longer do monkeys just abide in the far-away *jungle* — they hang out in our bedrooms, bathrooms, and nurseries. They've even become accustomed to our living rooms, leaping from the trees and onto our sofas. If your room hears the call of the wild, don't be afraid to go out on a limb!

*jungle*

Layers upon *layers* give our homes
a blanketed coziness, a cocooning effect.
For just as a cocoon is woven, we seek
to weave our home's next layer of
comfort each time we journey to flea
markets, antique shops, and fabric
boutiques. Our friend Judy is a master
of layering. She is, indeed, a cocoon
artist. At her request, her draperies
were removed and embellished with
gold metallic silk and tasseled trim.
Floral linen mixed with silk is pulled
back gently with a large tassel to emulate
a bountiful horn of plenty.

Newlyweds can exist almost purely and solely on one another. Their intense bond leaves little room for *interaction* with others. The purity of correct fabric selection harnesses this same intense bond, as shown here with the wedding of solid gold silk and gingham check silk. The trim adds just enough playfulness to this marriage to make it last until death do you part. Thanks to our newlyweds, Perry and Mary, for allowing us to witness their love for one another and their combined passion for a beautiful home.

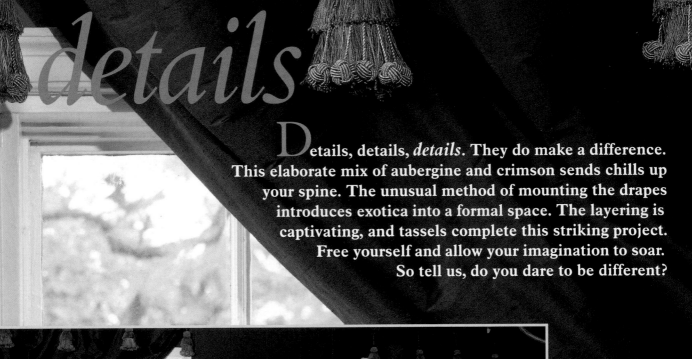

# details

$D$etails, details, *details*. They do make a difference. This elaborate mix of aubergine and crimson sends chills up your spine. The unusual method of mounting the drapes introduces exotica into a formal space. The layering is captivating, and tassels complete this striking project. Free yourself and allow your imagination to soar. So tell us, do you dare to be different?

Forget the locker room! Throw those nasty sneakers away! Our bachelor friend's pad will knock your socks off! This dining room inspired by the cigar room in North Carolina's fabled Biltmore House is intensely masculine, yet maintains warmth and culture. The warmth comes in part from the colors that reflect a great respect for the natural richness created by nature. Olive quilted charmeuse and Cheyenne rock suede convey earth tones in a *sophisticated* way, and the elegant hardware exudes stateliness and culture.

*sophisticated*

# Mixing Textures

*S*ince so much is offered, sometimes it's fun to choose more than one. For instance, we never order banana splits with just one topping, nor would we throw a dinner party only to invite one guest. We'd never grace a Chinese buffet to fill our plates with only sweet and sour chicken. When working on our designs, there are times when one fabric just won't do … so we mix it up! We put silks with chenille, we pair toile with floral, we add suede to printed linen, and we bounce polka dots off nubby chenille. Mixing textures gives greater dimension to your designs—they also energize and excite.

So, when selecting fabrics, take time to study texture, weaves, color variations, and patterns. Remember that combining fabrics always intensifies the design, and your rewards are a more customized finish.

plush

This impressive arch-head window (*left*) soars to fourteen feet. Attempting to work within a narrow budget, yet refusing to compromise our design goals, we confronted several obstacles. Due to the window's height, the yardage required would be immense. The room itself was grand in scale due to the height of the ceiling. We opted to create a treatment of mixed *textures* to infuse great style with a grand look. Crinkled opaque borders, in deep wine, cuff Greek key fabric, and a sheer petticoat ripples to the floor.

# textures

Imagine these simple panels (*opposite*) without the weave of silk. I can, because they hang in my gathering room. I had chosen this *plush* acanthus leaf chenille, thinking it would suffice on its own—I was so wrong. It looked weak, especially in the home of someone who designs window treatments for a living. The plain panels hung for several months, and finally, one day, I couldn't stand it any longer. I grabbed a chair, jumped up and jerked them down, then marched upstairs to the sewing room to begin breathing life into my drab drapes. The ruby silk is woven through a canal of five-inch-long buttonholes placed seven inches apart.

*I don't know if the shoemaker wears any shoes—all I care is that the drapery lady has pretty drapes!*

— Belinda

**K**iss the cook, or kiss the decorator of this kitchen! To shield the breakfast nook from the intense morning sun, floral linen backed with a thermal lining beautifully insulates. Can a box pleat hold the welcoming *surprise of silk*? Why not? The corner windows above the sink are sandwiched between two cabinets, but they're not ignored. Covered buttons reveal the surprise of silk once again. Silk in the kitchen? Why, of course!

*SILK*

# one of a

The combination of buttercream dupioni silk overlaid with a tone-on-tone silk plaid gives this monochromatic design the look of pure perfection. The valances were designed to be 24 inches deep and one-third wider than the windows.

By overstating the size and depth of the window, a theatrical stage is set for a ***one-of-a-kind*** drama. Multicolored glass beading traces the edge of the overlay, introducing another character in this multifaceted extravaganza.

*kind*

*trim*

**W**e trim a turkey. We trim a tree. We should always in some way *trim* our draperies. Take a look at these examples: they are trimmed in fabric, trimmed in cording, and trimmed also with fringes and beading. Mixing these textures promotes a finished look. It's like dotting an I or crossing a T. It's a bird! It's a plane! No, it's a finished drapery!

We want to encourage you to look not only at the pattern of a fabric, but at the texture as well. Think of it as planning a garden—you never want to plant just flowers. You also want to provide texture through trees, shrubs, and landscaping. Gardening and window treatments are all about *texture* and how one flourishes when combined with others.

# Appealing Hardware

## Make it or break it.

*Hardware can be the deciding factor in whether your window treatment goes for the gold or settles for second. Which place do you want to hold when you reach the finish line? The market has truly come alive with fabulous hardware. A few years ago the choices were limited. Now draperies are hung from fabulous woods—carved, scrolled, twisted, roped, and faux. The painted finishes dare to match any décor. Metals—blackened, bronzed, hammered, aged, and forged—are everywhere. Even the extremes— from fabric- or faux-finished PVC pipe to exotic bamboo treated with fire, earth, and water—are offered. Don't dismiss the unusual, such as candle wall sconces, decorative cup hooks, fence post finials, plant brackets, or any other artful option you may desire. Finally, finials if you so choose are gilded, molded, faux, carved, blown, and crackled.*

*When exploring your hardware options, don't forget to seek out your local hardware stores, craft and hobby shops, flea markets, antique and accessory shops. There are amazing finds out there, for those of us who shop with our creative eyes wide open.*

Becky really allowed herself to be free on this one. It's so refreshing and so *stimulating* to see drapery hanging from something so-o-o-o-o original. It almost (but not quite!) has a pretentious attitude about it. When you look out from the breakfast table, these stationary panels frame a golf course view. Intended as candle sconces, this hardware has stolen the show.

*stimulating*

*You don't mind if I steal your idea, do you, Becky?*

—Belinda

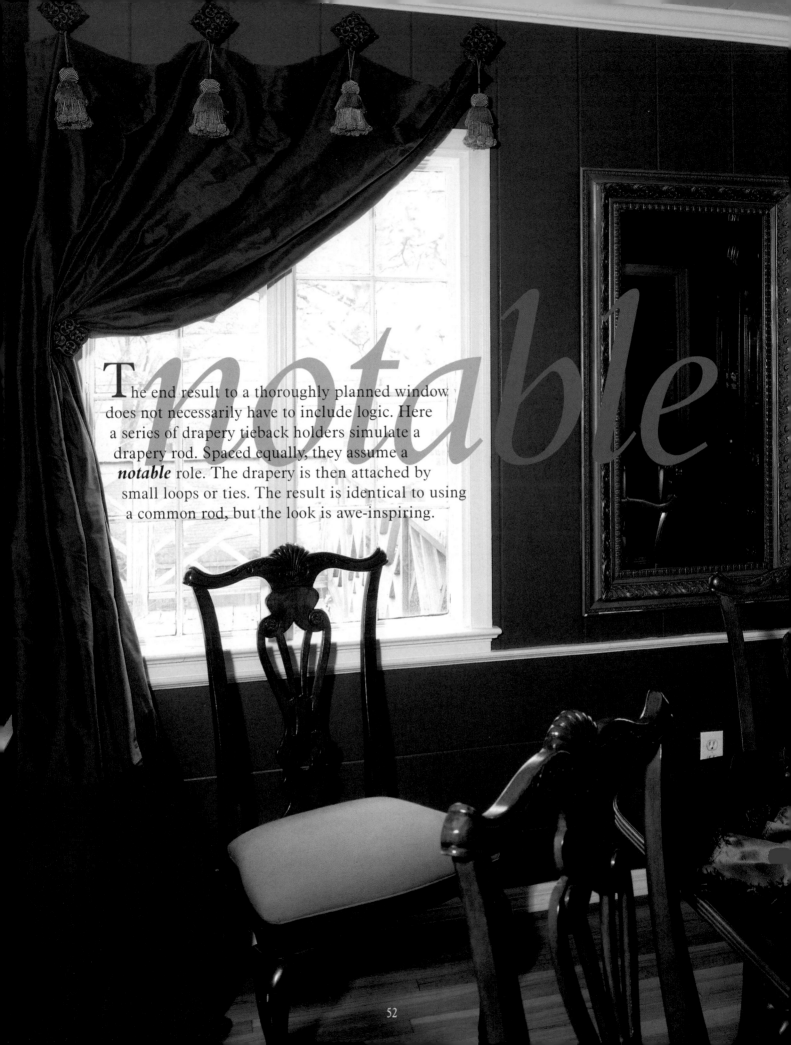

*notable*

The end result to a thoroughly planned window does not necessarily have to include logic. Here a series of drapery tieback holders simulate a drapery rod. Spaced equally, they assume a **notable** role. The drapery is then attached by small loops or ties. The result is identical to using a common rod, but the look is awe-inspiring.

In our homes, nothing is sacred. We cannot fully disclose to you how many times we have cut wooden bed rails apart for a drapery project and hoped the mattress would not fall through the frame, or removed the coffee mugs to place the *cup hooks* in a much worthier place, or cut up our husbands' shirts or ties in a fit of inspiration. As you see with this simple yet imaginative treatment *(below)*, cup hooks hold their own.

# CUP HOOKS

Macramé wood beads for trim, suede for the cuffs, fruited fabric filled with grapes and pomegranates in a spicy Indian red, and checkerboard drawer pulls are just the recipe for this piquant kitchen. The elegantly trimmed window provided a wonderful frame for this design. The three key ingredients that are paramount in this *succulent* blue-ribbon winner are beads, suede, and pulls.

**H**and-forged iron firmly supports these exquisite silk panels. The beautiful music room full of family heirlooms declares an air of aristocracy. Iron hardware has become increasingly popular these days. Its rough-hewn aspect validates any accommodation. When hanging such heavy apparatus, you must always remember to substantially secure it.

*hand-forged iron*

# garden

Symmetry is everything in this couple's Floridian breakfast room. The octagonal shape of the room, joined with the expansive height of the ceiling, sent us searching for unusual hardware. How about a Saturday morning trip to the local **garden** shop for drapery hardware? Exactly! Brass or iron? The choice wasn't difficult, but hanging this treatment would be. The over-sized watercolor-print panels add an impressive presence to the room when suspended from decorative plant brackets. Not only do the brackets add architectural elements, they also lend great dimension to the overall design.

58

**T**he hardware chosen for this traditional living space is treated bamboo with a *tortoiseshell* finish. This finish is derived from a 3,000-year-old technique originating in China that uses fire, earth, and water to create the mottled effect. Placing the rod at the ceiling line allows the room the advantage of all eight feet. This in turn balances the large scale of a grand piano and overstuffed chenille upholstery. This hardware boldly instills culture, and you won't even need an interpreter!

*tortoiseshell*

We have a responsibility to our Mother Earth. Hopefully, each of us participates in one or more acts of kindness, such as recycling or composting. Using PVC pipes as drapery rods is cost-effective, saves wood, and is a very *creative* medium to work with. Here we have PVC shirred with fabric *(top, right)* and also wrapped with fabric *(bottom)*. While you're at it, don't toss out those wood scraps. Wrap a wood piece in fabric *(top, left)* and hang a treatment from it. Check out your local hardware store—there's a project waiting for you!

*creative*

**G**reat challenges are often the catalyst for great achievements in life. The same can be said for challenging windows. Upon arriving to hang the draperies for this window, we discovered the degree of difficulty we were facing. There was no room for a center bracket and no place to support a ladder. So ... we boldly cut the long rod into pieces, placing 24-inch lengths on each side of the window and capping the inner ends of the rods with just a ball finial. On the outer ends, the original fancier finials were attached. Even though you may be unsure of a solution to an unforeseen dilemma, trust the *opportunities* that great challenges offer. Just do it!

O P P O R T U N I T Y

# Accessorizing Windows

**W**hat would a room be without accessories?
They are indeed the individuality of the room,
the cosmetics that set one room apart from another.
Accessories will change the mood or even the continent.
Do you like the flavor of Morocco or a taste of the
Orient? Do you crave the great outdoors or the feeling
of a cozy cabin? Window accessories can assist you in
achieving the ambience you most desire. Your senses
will be overwhelmed as you explore all your options
for decking out your drapes. There are large crystal
balls that properly sit on golden carved bases, but
when placed on the ends of a drapery rod, they
glisten as diamonds set in 24-carat gold. There are
tortoiseshell finials and carved wooden tassels, fleurs-
de-lis, cherubs, and stars. Passementeries are as fancy
as the word that defines them. There are bullions and
fringes, chenille tassels and gimps, cording and
beading, the unusual and exotic—when added to
a window treatment, the ensemble is ultimate. As
a rule of thumb, accessories are always optional and
may drive up the cost, but you can embellish a little
or embellish a lot, spend a little or spend a lot.

Like mother, like daughter—the enjoyment is doubled when working with these two. Each woman's home reflects a paragon of Victorian splendor. For Andrea, her gracious Cape Cod is but a façade for the true nature of her home. The dining room is a fascinating green, soothing to the eye and spilling onto the drapery. The multicolored silk panels are embellished with deep triangles corded at the top and finished with tasseled trim. The *ornamentation* is then secured to the drape with silk-covered buttons. A straightforward panel thus becomes a show of Victorian elegance even Andrea's ancestors would be proud of.

*ornamentation*

Accents of gold bestow unto this guest bedroom the *majestic* regality it so well deserves, as antiquities fill every corner with abounding splendor. The exaggerated use of gold bullion fringe implies an impeccable richness, but at the same time offers an invitation for guests to embrace their surroundings.

*majestic*

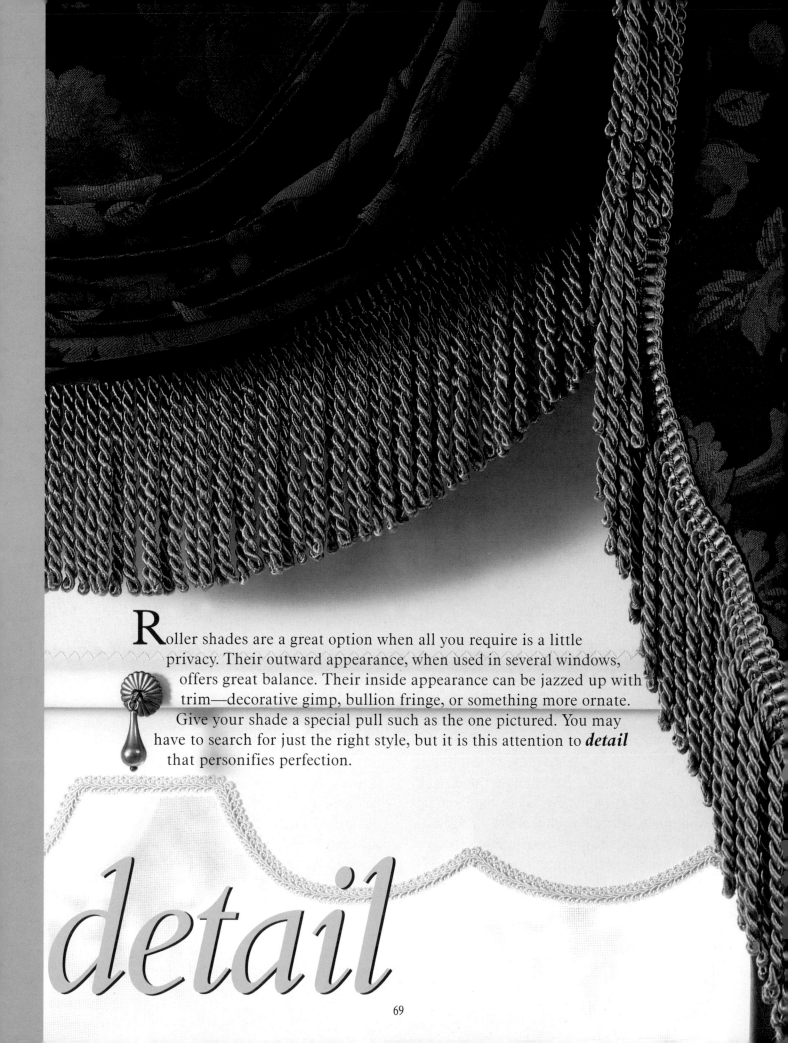

Roller shades are a great option when all you require is a little privacy. Their outward appearance, when used in several windows, offers great balance. Their inside appearance can be jazzed up with trim—decorative gimp, bullion fringe, or something more ornate. Give your shade a special pull such as the one pictured. You may have to search for just the right style, but it is this attention to *detail* that personifies perfection.

*detail*

Fretwork stone paths, stained glass, hydrangeas, even tiny little Johnny-jump-ups—your very senses are filled. You've lifted the latch on the ornate 100-year-old gate and made your way to the intricately detailed stained glass door. You hear the soothing chimes, but you don't remember the walk. Time for a moment has stood still. For this couple, detail is everything, and everything is nothing less than perfection. Every room in this Victorian palace has a story to be told. The breakfast room, as do most of the rooms, enjoys a lake view. The house sits on a tree-shaded lot, so we are always finding new ways to coax the light in. The metallic sheer treatments were the perfect complement for the sun and view. Light glistens in and the beaded trims become *sparkling jewels*. At dusk the transparency of the window evolves into something much more substantial. The design takes a stronger hold on the room. Double-faced tape, staples, and a board are all that is needed to create this design. Can't sew? You don't need to on this one. Not a stitch.

*sparkling jewels*

The brilliant colors of this pleated balloon shade *(below)* introduce an ethnic influence. The soft, billowy folds give way to a sort of Moroccan playfulness. The treasures of this spirited treatment are its tangerine and topaz tassels.

**T**his misplaced Texan's eclectic, Old-World style will *spice* up any room. Tobacco, nutmeg, maple sugar, rum, olive oil, and pomegranate—get the flavor? Five multi-trimmed banners provide an ethnic backdrop for a military family's mealtime sharing. Cording, glass and wood beads, and a combination of fabrics bring a rush of color into an already zesty kitchen.

spice

*great trim*

Laundry … the one chore there is never enough time for. It's the one thing, like taxes, that we must concede our wills to. We personally think that by envisioning your laundry room as pleasantly as possible, the chore becomes less dreaded. We offer these fun examples *(this page)* to lighten and brighten your washday engagement. The design should always be fun, with scalloped edges, themed fabric, and don't forget **great trim** and hardware. Slap on a pretty coat of paint to make your window pop, and before you know it, those washday blues will fade away!

America is blessed with rich, fertile soil that for generations has brought forth bountiful harvests that not only feed our diverse nation but also help sustain many others. Some of the massive plantations of yesteryear, complete with their beautiful homes, are still sprinkled throughout the countryside across this great land of ours, and sometimes those homes require a little tender, loving care. This **glorious** antebellum homesite *(right)* was reborn when inherited by the grandson. His love for the home's historical preservation and its integrity is evident in the restoration process. The draperies were also designed to sustain the true virtue of this Southern parlor. Panels of goldenrod damask trimmed with an ornate multi-tassel trim accent but do not overpower, for this splendid beauty stands on her own.

74

Three panels of sheer elegance ... this window's decadent look could be very costly to one's pocketbook. Superb fabric choices, though, guarantee you won't have to dip into your retirement fund. The body of the drape is made from very affordable fabric, but it's the accessories that impart richness to this design. One-and-one-half yards of embroidered silk provide an *exquisite* overlay. Dazzling, ornate buttons purchased at the local fabric store are essential elements for securing this ensemble.

*exquisite*

# Enhancing Ready-Mades

*Linen shops seem to be popping up all over. Linen means "thread or cloth made of flax; articles made of linen or of cotton, such as tablecloths, sheets, etc.," or at least so says my Webster's. Who would have thought you could get ideas for draperies from a dictionary? Sheets, tablecloths, linens, oh my! What a great idea for those of us whose lives are full of prioritizing and sacrificing something good for something better, something great for something greater. Ready-mades are so very adaptable, versatile, and moderately priced.*

*Just how infinite is your imagination? Because today's linens are not the same as when our younger selves used to climb in bed and throw the sheets over our heads to hide us from whatever our imaginations had conjured up—they are much more evolved. They have become cotton sateens with thread counts as high as 800 per inch. At that count, just toss the PJ's, for they won't feel near as good as the sheets. And if you can bear to pull those fine sheets off the bed, you can line them and hang them on your windows.*

*If you're looking for something different, try tablecloths, napkins, or tea towels from Country French, to Italian, to beautiful damask. Line them, maybe even interline them, and you've just added an elegant piece of décor to your room at half the cost. Department stores, boutiques, and discount outlet catalog stores are wonderful places to find the latest, greatest, or the discontinued. Remember when you buy a king-size sheet you are actually purchasing 6 yards of fabric. You do the math. You'll still have money for dinner and a movie. So if you've blown your budget on three rooms and you still have two more to go, try ready-mades, a pair of scissors, and oh yeah, your imagination.*

cottage

# garden

**T**his pageantry of floral linens has you believing you are asleep in a sun-filled *cottage garden*. With walls painted a parakeet green, you can almost see the blooms growing. Reworking flowery ready-made balloon shades added even more warmth to this bedroom.

The balloon shades were redesigned into single box-pleated valances and secured over multicolored plaid panels. A two-tone green woven check peeking out from the box pleat inserts provides the perfect final touch for this re-creation.

**O**ne would never imagine this bedding was purchased at a discount store. Coupled with coordinating fabric, this master bedroom *masterpiece* was unleashed. A covered headboard provides an impressive focal point, while two windows complete the symmetry. The soft, pleated valance and the tone-on-tone sheer ensure that only her decorator knows for sure what's custom and what's not.

*masterpiece*

# OPULENCE

**R**avishing in red. Just a glimpse of the color really heats things up. This room, very appropriately, is called the Red Room. It is the pinnacle of enhancing ready-mades, and as you can see, there need be no end to the *opulence* one can achieve. Because this window is placed in an alcove, it automatically becomes the focal point. The two purchased panels that make up the crown were cut and remade to the appropriate design. An inexpensive opaque crinkled sheer made into a balloon shade provides dazzling contrast for the dollar. Remember when searching for and selecting fabrics the old adage, "You get what you pay for" gets thrown out the window. Look for contrast, color combinations, and textures when enhancing your ready-mades. If you feel the need to splurge, you may add all the bells and whistles your little heart desires. Just remember … bells and whistles may cost you the farm.

Something as simple as **banding** turned an imported tablecloth into a delightful and interesting addition to this second-story landing. The complementary fabric has an iridescent nature and provides a rolled cuff at the top. We're sure after seeing this creation, Grandmother's linens will never look the same.

*banding*

A newly renovated *vintage* kitchen deserves vintage curtains newly renovated. A honeymoon to Martha's Vineyard a few years past provided this homeowner a bargain she couldn't pass up. Reviving antique textiles is always a noteworthy task. As with this pair of fruited fancies, a simple addition to their length, gingham covered buttons, and this vested vintage once again enjoys a sunlit view.

This pastel patchwork valance *(left)* sits so pretty over a pair of cotton plaid sheers, and purple daisies seem to be popping up all over! This multi-textured treatment was a continuing process, with the first addition being that of the purchased plaid sheers. The custom patchwork cornice, complete with ruffles and ball trim, became the second **layer**. The final layer of a ready-made embossed sheer that allowed the room to play peekaboo with the light … boo!

Have you ever strolled down the aisle of a catalog discount store, or any discount store for that matter, and unfolded the wonderful tablecloths and napkins ready to be remade into anything your imagination can dream up? Picked up for a song, these three Country French napkins *(below)*—**layered** and hung on hooks—are far better off enhancing this window than tossed into the washer.

# Bathroom Break

Probably the most challenging article to find for a home is a shower curtain. With the nine-foot ceilings they are building in new homes, why aren't the shower curtains getting longer? Regardless if your home has eight-foot ceilings, or boasts of nine feet or greater, it seems when examining our choices for shower curtains or bath treatments we tend to just settle. Those of us who refuse defeat, very diligently continue our search. Besides, our baths should receive as much noteworthy attention as every other room in our homes.

We find that placing things in our bathrooms—things that normally say, "We don't belong"—makes visits to those rooms much more relaxing and enjoyable. Every room deserves to have a beautiful environment. Soft coverings for bath openings or windows will certainly extend a warmer invitation to linger just a little longer as we powder our noses.

Lavender linen, rosebuds, and snow-white chenille … it's a genius collaboration of shabby and chic. The chenille shower curtain was purchased at a discount center and provides the body of the curtain. The lavender linen adds length at the hemline, while also enhancing the rosebud fabric to make a pretty border at the top. A row of covered buttons perfect this *touchable* style.

touchable

Archways, tunnels, and alcoves lead to *intriguing* places and spaces. This home is a mélange of openings offering the unexpected to those whose curiosity is yet to be satisfied. In this arched bath opening hang two bluebird-colored silk panels purchased at a home improvement store. A dramatic layer of pintucked kiwi silk adds length, and chenille fringe beautifully separates the fabrics. The small window's treatment begins with the same blue silk overlaid with an embroidered fabric. Above this simple roman shade a hand-carved pediment provides an eyecatching focal point.

*intriguing*

Out with the old and in with the new! Ranch-style homes are so much a part of Americana, but many these days are being transformed. For this particular home *(above)*, it received one of the finest face-lifts Becky and I have ever witnessed—a total custom look. The bath, however, was to be part of the phase-two transformation. So, for now, a new coat of paint, wallpaper, and a couple of great fabrics add spark to this 1950's-era bath. Remember, when breathing life into a dated room, fabrics can resuscitate and **rejuvenate**.

Stars and stripes are forever, and it's the stripes in this bath *(opposite)* that say more than the traditional whisper we usually lend an ear to. To promote **instant energy**, bold hues of aqua, raspberry, melon, and gold storm this 1950's bath. The tasseled triangle valance is a splendid design, as it makes a big statement for a small window.

instant energy

Beautiful embroidered sheers lighten this pretty powder room. Thermal lining adds not only privacy but a layer of protection as well. The wispy swags add a *lighthearted* layer, while the novel cascades on the windows make things really swing.

Modern baths are frequently encased in a number of elements such as marble, tile, granite, or wood panels that, while providing elegance, often result in harsh, cold lines. Thick glass blocks in this bath *(opposite)* provide diffused light that requires softening with the use of fabric. Supple gathers prove the perfect approach to this neutral bath. Bullion trim adds luxuriousness, a distinct richness. The sheer metallic panels gently fuse the bath and shower area together. The finale comes when the mixture of hard elements is combined with soft furnishings to provide an oasis for body, mind, and soul.

softening

A historical neighborhood is the scene for this makeover. With two growing sons, Ryan and Reed, *lively* colors in electric blue, sunburst yellow, and crisp white were introduced to hopefully persuade the young boys in from playtime to bath time. The foremost need in the bathroom was to conceal the uncoordinated bath surround. To begin the process, two shower curtains were purchased: one white and one yellow. We cut the top from the yellow one to provide length to the bottom of the white one—what was meant to hang from rings now hangs from buttons. Remember when purchasing something to be redesigned, look at every aspect of its design and imagine how it can be reworked to your advantage.

LIVELY

A young family has so much to look forward to: planning, saving, moving, and moving again or renovating. With one child toddling about and another on the way, this couple's first little cottage was splitting at the seams.

Soon after moving, the renovation began on their new two-story dwelling. The kitchen redo came first and the bath followed close behind. A retro look for the first-level bath was decided upon. Lime green, aqua, and khaki— sounds fun, looks great! To keep costs down, two drapery panels with expensive-looking extra-large grommets were purchased. Aqua fabric added length to the original curtains, taking this new shower treatment to greater height. Box pleats in coordinating white duck fabric *add a kick* to this geometrical design package.

*add a kick*

This 1950's bath recently encountered a major facelift. The owner's marvelous *classical* taste prevails throughout her home, and her renovated bath received the same fine treatment. From paint to paper, drawer pulls to whirlpool, not one gem was left unpolished. The soft furnishings offer true classical design. Straight lines are never mundane when a variety of textures are introduced. Would we forget the tiny, recessed window? Never! A roman shade, a valance, and a toile sheer add the layers of privacy required for a serene bath.

C  L  A  S  S  I  C  A  L

# SOLITAIRE

**Diamonds are a girl's best friend … but in this marbled bath, the drapery runs a close second. After seeing the black dupioni silk with overlays of embroidered silk, the homeowner instantly chose this treatment as the *solitaire* most desired.**

# Kidding Around

There is nothing more monumental or life changing than the birth of a baby. I'll never forget the day Becky shared with me—over lunch—her extraordinary glimpse into childbirth, when she witnessed the birth of her dear friend's baby Kate. Her extremely vivid play-by-play explanation was like listening to a sportscaster during a big game. Fortunately, long after we've survived childbirth, we spend countless hours in the nursery loving, cuddling and caring for our new bundles of joy.

Nurseries have become quite diverse in design. Walls with beautiful scenes artfully depict everything from classic movies to nursery rhymes come to life. Fabric walls accented with grosgrain ribbon and colorful buttons invite the whimsical. Windows with room-darkening treatments provide soft, low light for long, relaxing naps. Treatments of choice would be billowing balloons, roman shades with fancy valances, or soft cornices over embroidered sheers. All these, and more, allow you to control the light and ensure naptime is a happy time.

In a room so dramatically adorned, this princess-to-be will be sleeping in high cotton. Multi-textured panels softly frame the window and whimsical baby bed. The crib, set in its own alcove, takes center stage. The window treatment creates a mirroring alcove—the triangle valance projects 21" from the window, allowing the panel "walls" to drop from the ceiling to complete the effect. Ribbons forming a harlequin design are secured with wooden daisies on raspberry-washed walls to add a lighthearted backdrop to this *fanciful* fairytale finale.

# fanciful

Three little kittens lost their mittens
Eating a Christmas pie.
Peter, Peter, pumpkin eater,
kissed the girls and made them cry.

Precocious plaids and bouncy bubbles release a fairy tale spell on this kindergartner's imaginary kingdom. "Dog ears" tie this fanciful festoon, and the ruffled edge makes playtime an *enchanting* time.

enchanting

Mother Goose and Doctor Seuss,
Ring around the rosie.
Here a moo, there a moo,
A pocket full of posies.

**D**aisies are coming up all over in this gender-friendly nursery turned toddler's room. Apple green, engine red, sunshine yellow, and periwinkle blue are the childlike jumble of a colored page in Kenneth's real-life coloring book. His room employs an ***imaginative*** scheme as daisy-pleated balloons were festooned with fanciful French tassels. An appliquéd organdy panel adorned with ABC's and 123's swings high above the antique trundle bed.

Zebras, giraffes, and monkeys bequeath a juvenile atmosphere to this baby's room. And rightfully so, for this is Bailey's nursery—her special abode. English smocked balloons dance across the windows, and matching ruffled linens fit for a tiny princess give her a *comfy* place to lay her little head.

COMFY

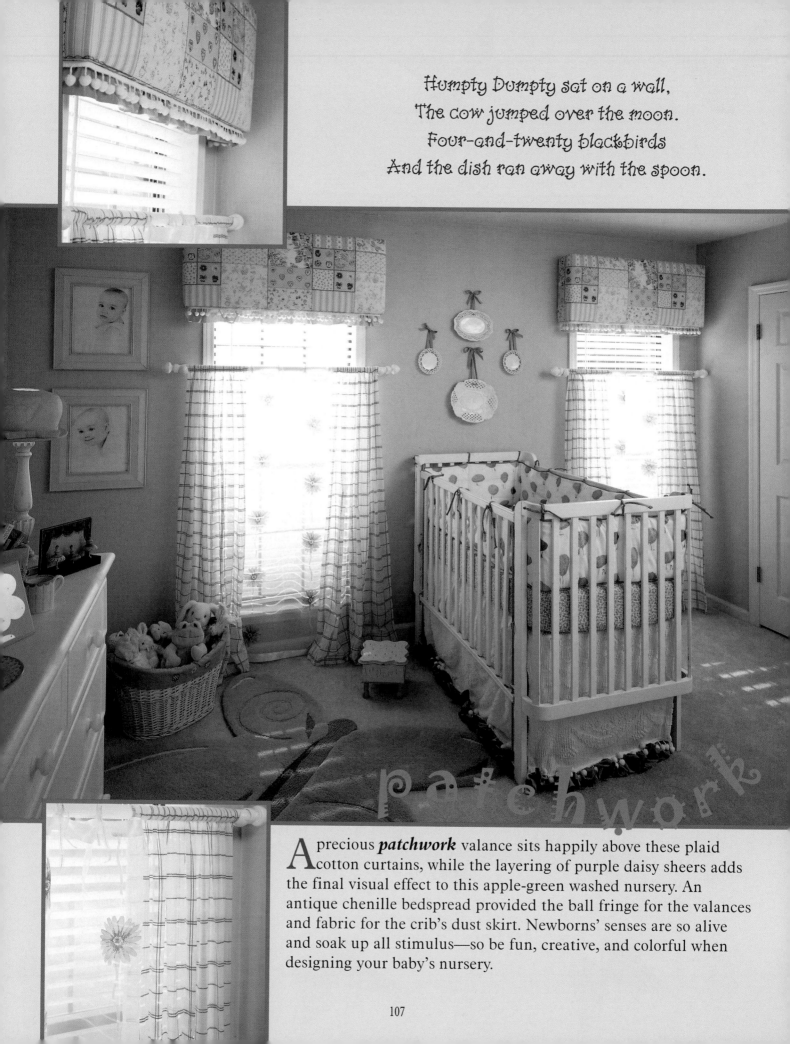

Humpty Dumpty sat on a wall,
The cow jumped over the moon.
Four-and-twenty blackbirds
And the dish ran away with the spoon.

A precious **patchwork** valance sits happily above these plaid cotton curtains, while the layering of purple daisy sheers adds the final visual effect to this apple-green washed nursery. An antique chenille bedspread provided the ball fringe for the valances and fabric for the crib's dust skirt. Newborns' senses are so alive and soak up all stimulus—so be fun, creative, and colorful when designing your baby's nursery.

Frogs, dragonflies, and beetles aren't the recipe for a witch's brew, but for a delightful window awning in a baby's nursery. A quaint little garden was planted outside the window for mom and baby to enjoy. As baby grew into a toddler, the garden also grew. Our *happy insects* seem to be as at home on the awning as they are in the garden.

# Falling Pennies

At some point in our lives, we finally shed the cocoons that sheltered us for so many years. Those parental coverings where we felt so safe and secure are gone. We are ready to spread our own beautiful wings, using all the excitement, enthusiasm, and energy that could one day send mankind soaring past the moon to Mars or light-years away to explore another galaxy … and all we really long for is a good-looking curtain. Now, if only we had NASA's budget!

This is when we need to withdraw into stealth mode. We need not share with our friends, acquaintances, or loved ones how we pulled off such a drop-dead gorgeous window treatment, bedding ensemble, or slipcovered sofa. Or tell how we found 50 dollar-a-yard fabric for next-to-nothing, or secured yardage that was once an exclusive to a certain famous designer. Or should we? Why not? After all, sharing is half the fun. When looking for cheap fixes and inexpensive chic, remember shopping and store hopping is what it's all about. To share a little secret with you … the early bird does gets the worm. So, unless pennies start falling from heaven, happy hunting!

Decorating a first home is a daunting task, especially when the home has large, *expansive* windows. Knowing that providing covering for windows might be costly, Stacey and Brent asked if we could find something reasonable. Our task paid off when we were able to locate 33 yards of a great waffle-like fabric at a very reasonable price. This texture added a striking contrast to their Tuscan-finished walls. Brent, establishing himself as a do-it-yourselfer, saved even more cost by hanging the draperies himself. After the completion of the living room, these newlyweds were making plans for a nursery.

EXPANSIVE

A lavender damask shade provides a beautiful background for a 1920's bath *(below)* — elegant and ***romantic*** when raised, very beneficial when lowered. For an intoxicating and stimulating presentation, try a balloon.

*romantic*

**S**oft, butterfly-like valances *romanticize* these newlyweds' master suite. Their department-store bedding is enhanced with Euro shams made from an exclusive fabric etched with a crested "V". We purchased the fabric at a local discounted-and-discontinued outlet; only the savvy shopper who's up on the textile scene would recognize such a gem. There are jewels out there to be found. It's like digging for diamonds—you never know when you'll unearth a worthy find.

Need to make those pennies stretch? Try burlap. If caught on sale, it may be purchased for as little as two dollars a yard. Line it appropriately and you'll have to look twice to realize *it isn't raw silk.*

*it isn't raw silk*

# week end PROJECT

Natural reed is a great material to work with. Its versatility is endless: fencing, floral arrangements, totes, photo frames, even furniture. If you desire an Eastern approach in your decorating, reed garden fencing is a must. Packaged in 6' x 15' bundles, this fencing is a bargain shopper's dream. We made this reed shade, complete with a decorative valance and pulley system that allows the shade to be raised or lowered. All you need to make your own shade is a 1x6 board, L-brackets, utility scissors, wire cutters, pulley, string, and of course, fencing.

We guarantee this to be a great *weekend project*.

Living through a home renovation is an overwhelming reality. One couple once told us they sat on lawn chairs in the family room for months. Another couple, while renovating their kitchen, used an ice chest in place of a refrigerator and an electric skillet as a stove. Thank goodness they all got around to decorating their windows. For Craig and Alisa, their master bedroom and bath were included in their renovation. Since the bath became a part of their bedroom, draperies were designed to incorporate both. Planned exclusively for privacy, these draperies shut out the world and the light, and muffled the sound.

Open floor plans *indulge* our freedom to feel uninhibited. Exposed baths, at times though, make us feel a little overexposed. If a door seems to be too much, try a soft drapery. When lined, interlined, and gently pulled back, it becomes a dramatic entrance. Forget the hinges—hang a rod, toss on the tassels, and let the bubbles begin!

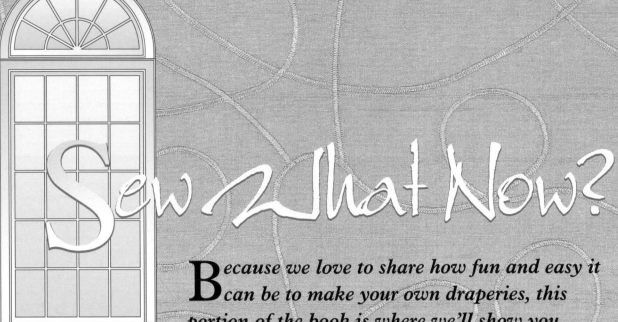

# Sew What Now?

**B**ecause we love to share how fun and easy it can be to make your own draperies, this portion of the book is where we'll show you some colorful palettes of fabrics, textures, hardware, and accessories that are sure to inspire your next design. You'll also find instructions for several of our favorite window treatments, such as a variety of panel treatments and valances, and even a reed fencing shade. Don't worry if you aren't a master seamstress. These projects are ones that most anyone can complete!

At the end of a busy day when you walk through the door of your home, toss your keys and let out a deep sigh, we want you to be able to say, as Frank sang so many times, "I Did It My Way."

# The Math Matters

Whether you like it or not, the math matters. The success of your drapery depends upon how accurately you measure your window and how well you plot out those measurements before you cut the first piece of fabric. First, you need to determine how the treatment will function, how it will be mounted, and how full and how long it will be. Then, make a roadmap—a list or a sketch of the attributes of your treatment. Use your roadmap to record everything about your project.

*Outside Width*

*Inside Width*

*Stackback*

*Floor-to-Ceiling*

## TO MEASURE FOR AN INSIDE MOUNTED TREATMENT

Measure the inside width of the window at three different places: from left to right at the top, center, and bottom. Always use the shortest measurement. Measure the inside height at three different places: from top to bottom at left edge, center, and right edge to get your finished height. Always use your longest measurement.

## TO MEASURE FOR AN OUTSIDE MOUNTED TREATMENT

Measure the exact width of the area to be covered in three different places as you would for an inside mount. You will want to determine how far your treatments will stack back on each side of your window to get this measurement. Deciding on how your treatment will be hung and where the hemline falls will determine your finished height.

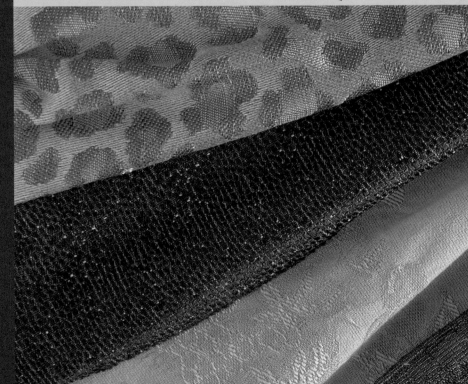

# silks

# Selecting

# wovens

# prints

# Fabrics

# sheers

Our sampling of fabrics will make you head straight for the fabric store to look, touch, dream, and compare. Beginning a new project always has its challenges—choosing the perfect fabric is one of the most fun!

# Combining

# Textures

Mingling different textures
is the hallmark of an exciting
design. Each of these photos
tells a story, a story about texture.
Look how we combined smooth
with nubby, sheer with opaque,
shiny with matte, hard with soft.
See how the trims pull all the
colors of the design together.
Notice how unexpected
combinations can harmonize.

We love trims of every style, material, and hue,
don't you? Add a trim, a fringe, a ribbon, a tassel,
or all of the above to your design and it instantly looks lush.

# More, More, More!

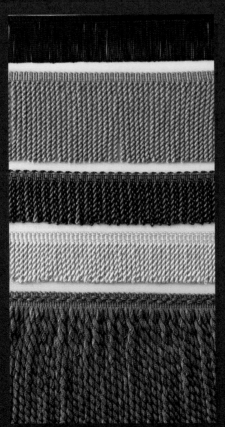

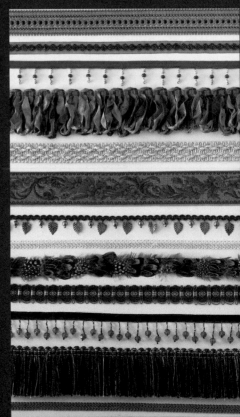

What your window treatment hangs from can be just as exciting as the fabric it's made from. Rods of every material, size, and color can be fancied up with fascinating finials. Rings to hang your draperies from come in all sizes and shapes. Looking for hardware with a twist? Hooks, tieback holders, knobs, or even buttons may be just the answer.

Hang It All

# The Perfect Panel

If you can master the simple sewing required to make a plain, flat panel, you are well on your way to being able to make any drapery you desire. Here we show you our favorite way to make a plain panel (very useful when working with sheers!) and how to make a lined one.

These days, we rarely use panels with rod pockets because of all the fabulous rings and clips available that make any treatment look custom. So, in essence, a panel is just a rectangle of fabric with hemmed edges.

We usually allow 2" double hems (allow 4" of fabric for the hem) on the side and a 5" double hem (allow 10" of fabric) on the bottom edge. At the top edge, we like to use 2" triple hems to provide a really sturdy area to attach rings. Hems are highly variable, however. You may need to change them to fit your project.

## The Plain Panel

**See some examples:** Plain panels are used on pages 16, 17, 28, 44, 82, and 93. Many of these panels are made from sheer fabric.

**Make the plan:** You'll use ½" seam allowances when sewing. Mount your rod at the window at the desired height and place the rings on the rod. *Find the cut length* – Measure from the bottom of the ring to where you wish the panel to end to determine finished length. Use following formula to get the length of fabric to cut.

Cut length = Finished length + 6" (for top hem)
+ 10" (for double hem at bottom)

*Find the cut width* – Determine how wide you wish the finished panel to be. This will depend on how many panels you are using for a window and how much fullness you wish the panel to have when placed on the rod. Use the following formula to get the width of fabric to cut. (Depending on the width of the panel you are using, you may be required to piece two or more fabric widths together to get the correct size. Don't forget to add in the seam allowances when you are cutting these pieces.)

Cut width = Finished width + 4" (for left double hem) + 4" (for right double hem)

**Cut your fabric:** Use the measurements from your "plan" to cut your panel. (If you need to use more than one width of fabric, you'll need to cut the required number of widths needed, then sew them together.)

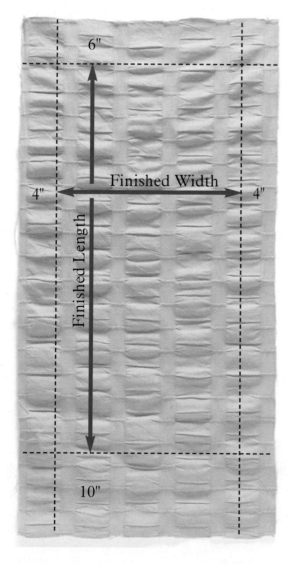

**Hem the bottom edge:** Press the bottom edge 10" to the wrong side. Open up the fabric, then fold the raw edge to the inside to meet the crease, forming a 5"W hem. Stitch the hem in place using the blindstitch on your sewing machine or handstitch in place. **Make the top hem:** Press the top edge 2" to the wrong side; press 2" to wrong side again, then 2" once more. Blindstitch in place.

**Make the side hems:** Press the right edge 4" to the wrong side. Open up the fabric, then proceed as before to make a 2"W double hem. Repeat the same process for the left side edge.

**Add reinforcement areas:** We strongly recommend you add reinforcement areas where you'll attach drapery hooks. This may not be necessary when making a sheer, but heavier fabrics will hang better when this improvement is added. Mark the placement of the hooks along the top edge. Beginning at the top edge at each mark, stitch a 1½"L x ½"W rectangle. Insert the drapery hook in the rectangle through several fabric layers on the back of the panel and know your drapery will be well supported.

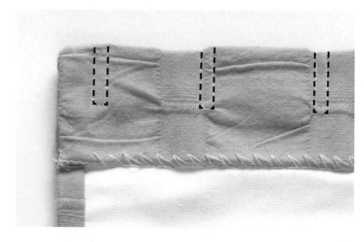

Guess what? You're done!! All you need to do is give the entire panel a quick press, then hang it on the rod and enjoy your wonderful creation!

# The Lined Panel

Making a lined panel is similar to making an unlined one, but you'll need to make a few adjustments in your measurements. These formulas are based on a panel with a 2"W side hem on each edge and a 5"W hem at the bottom. Lining a panel can make a huge difference in your treatment. It adds body and weight to a treatment, making it more substantial and luxurious.

**See some examples:** Lined panels are shown on pages 10, 12, 18, 32, 51, 66, 75, 94, and 116.

**Changes in the plan:** *Find the cut panel length –* Determine the finished length as you did in making The Plain Panel (page 126) and use the same formula above to determine the cut length of your panel fabric. *Find the cut panel width –* Determine the finished width of the panel and use the following formula (Don't forget, if you are piecing multiple widths to get the finished width, add in those extra seam allowances.):

Cut width = Finished width + 2" (for left hem)
+ 2" (for right hem)
+ 1" (for seam allowances)

**Cut your fabrics:** Cut your panel fabric to these measurements, piecing widths if needed. Cut the lining fabric 4" narrower than the width of your panel and 14" shorter than the panel length.

**Hem the bottom edges:** Make a 2"W double hem on the bottom edge of the lining. Make a 5"W double hem on the bottom edge of the panel fabric.

**Stitch the side edges:** Place the lining and panel right sides together with one side edge aligned and the bottom of the lining 1" above the bottom edge of the panel. Sew the matched side edges together using a ½" seam allowance, then match the remaining side edges and sew them. Turn right side out. Press the panel and lining flat with the lining centered. This will form 2"W panel fabric "hems" on the lining side.

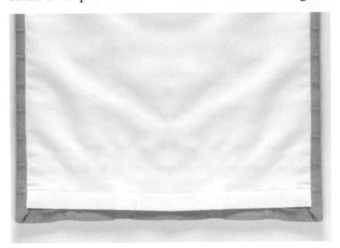

**Finish the job:** Press the top edge of the panel to the wrong side as you did in making a plain panel. This should cover the top raw edge of the lining. Add the reinforcement areas in the same manner (they are <u>essential</u> when making a lined panel) and you're done!!

**A note about interlining:** Sometimes, one extra layer of lining can make the difference. Sandwiching a thermal lining or a blackout lining between your drapery fabric and its lining can make your drapery more functional. Treat interlining the same as lining fabric, making sure to make it just slightly shorter than the lining.

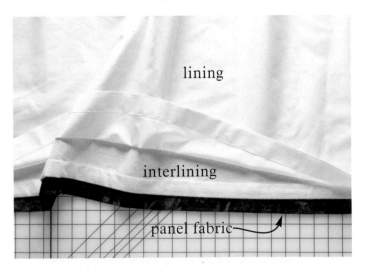

lining

interlining

panel fabric

# The Woven Trim Panel

**Make the buttonholes:** Start with a finished flat panel. Determine where the woven trim will be placed. Mark 5"L buttonholes, evenly spaced, across the panel. Work the buttonholes and cut them open. Remove the markings.

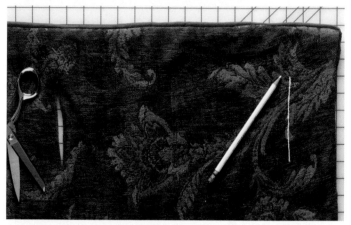

**Make the fabric trim:** Cut a 15"W strip of your contrasting lightweight fabric several inches longer than the width of the panel (the wider the panel, the more extra inches you'll need). You may need to piece several lengths together to get the correct length. Finish the edges of the strip.

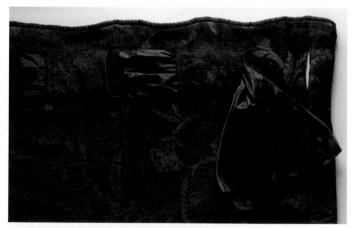

If your sewing machine can make buttonholes, you can make a little bit of magic! All you need is a plain finished panel, made by you or purchased, and a contrasting fabric, preferably lightweight, for weaving!

**Finish the job:** Weave the fabric strip through the buttonholes, making sure not to pull so tightly that you gather up the panel. Secure the ends of the strip on the back of the panel using a few stitches.

# The Banded Panel

This panel starts off with a plain, flat piece of fabric. Coordinating strips of fabrics and trims are added to one side edge (usually the side that goes toward the center of the window) to create a drapery with lots of visual punch.

These instructions tell you how to add cording, a shirred (gathered) fabric band, and a flat fabric band to the body of your primary panel fabric. Trims are then added. The width measurements given for each strip are those used on the panel in the photograph here and on page 26. You may need to make adjustments for your panel.

**Gather your supplies:** You need fabric for primary portion of your panel; fabric for shirred portion of panel (make sure that this fabric is not too stiff or heavy) and thin, strong cord or nylon line; fabric for contrast portion of panel; cording; fabric for lining; sewing supplies; fabric glue; double-sided adhesive tape.

**Cut your primary panel:** Cut, then sew, as many widths of primary fabric together as needed to make a panel 16" narrower and 4½" longer than the desired finished size.

**Add cording:** Sew the cording to the side edge only of the primary panel.

**Add a shirred band:** Cut, then sew, enough 9"W strips of the shirred band fabric so that you can piece together a single strip that is 3 times the length of the cut measurement of your primary panel. (Example: If your panel's cut length is 103", you will need a 309" strip.) To gather, place the thin cord ½" from one long edge of the strip and zigzag stitch over the cord to hold the cord in place, being careful not to stitch into the cord.

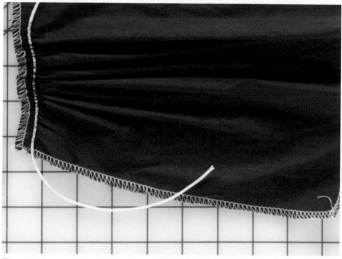

Do this on both long edges of the strip. Then pull the cords to gather each long edge to the primary panel length measurement, making sure the gathers are evenly distributed along both edges. Secure the cords at top and bottom, then sew one edge of the shirred strip to the edge of the primary panel, sandwiching the cording in between.

**Add a contrast band:** Cut a 10½"W strip of contrast fabric. Ideally, you should cut this piece from the lengthwise grain of fabric in a single piece. Sew this to the raw edge of the shirred piece.

**Add trims:** Use double-sided tape or fabric glue to attach a length of trim over the seam between the shirred band and the flat band and another length at least 1" from edge of contrast band.

**Add cording to top of panel:** Sew cording to top edge of panel.

**Line the panel:** Cut lining fabric 1" narrower than panel width and 1" shorter than panel length. Make a 2"W double hem on bottom edge of lining. Press bottom edge of panel 4" to wrong side; blindstitch or hand-stitch in place. Sew side edges of panel and lining together. Sew top edge of lining and panel together, making sure lining is centered between side edges. Turn, and press.

# The Cuffed Panel

A cuffed panel is easy to make, but creates an elaborate design splash! Basically, it's just a panel with an extra-wide hem at the top. Use a rod with rings for mounting. Remember that adding length creates the illusion of height in a room. Consider mounting the rod quite a bit above the window.

**See some examples:** Cuffed panels are shown on pages 23, 34, 54, 63, and 112.

**Cut the fabric:** Mount your rod at the window. Hang the rings on the rod so that you can determine the finished length of the panel. Add 10" (for the bottom hem) and 18" (for the top cuff) to equal your cut length. Determine the finished width of the panel and add 3" (for hems). Cut panel fabric to the determined size, piecing width if needed. Cut lining fabric 2" narrower and 22" shorter than panel fabric.

**Finish side and bottom edges:** Finish the top edge of the panel fabric. See The Lined Panel, page 127, to hem bottom edges of panel and lining and attach lining to side edges of panel. The top edge of the lining should be about 14" below top edge of drapery fabric.

**Start the cuff:** Fold the side edges of the top portion of the panel to the wrong side so they are even with the rest of the panel; press. Fold

the top edge of the panel 15" to the lining side of the panel; press.

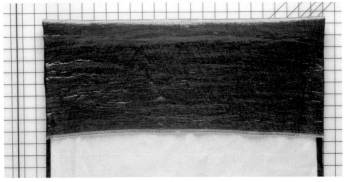

**Finish the cuff:** On wrong side of panel, mark placement of rings along finished edge of panel fabric. See The Plain Panel, page 126, to add reinforced areas at each mark.

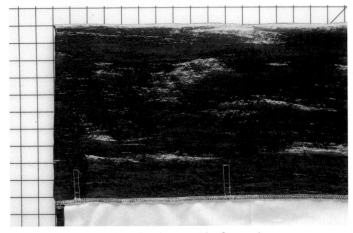

Insert drapery hooks into reinforced areas through all layers of fabrics.

Attach rings, and "cuff" excess fabric at top of panel to the right side.

# The Napkin Topper

A napkin topper is the easiest of all draperies to make! Simply purchase napkins that work well in the room you are designing and fold them in half diagonally to make triangles. Make sure to purchase more napkins than you think you'll need! There's no guarantee that you'll be able to find them the next time you're out shopping.

or you can sew a rod pocket across the top of the folded napkins to create a gathered look. You can always personalize the napkins with trims.

Your napkins can be stapled onto a mounting board, clipped to drapery rings, or attached to wall-mounted hooks using a few quick stitches. They can also drape over a simple tension rod,

# The Triangle Valance

A simple valance made of triangular-shaped pieces is quite striking at almost any window.

**See some examples:** Triangle valances are shown on pages 29, 93, and 103.

**Gather your supplies:** You need 1x4 lumber for mounting board; L-brackets; fabric for the triangles; cording (optional); lining fabric; staple gun.

**Make the mounting board:** Cut a piece of lumber to fit your window. Wrap the mounting board "gift-wrap" style with lining fabric, securing fabric with staples on what will become the top of the mounting board.

**Make the plan:** Decide the total number of triangles your design will have, making sure it is an odd number. The triangles will be placed in two rows on the mounting board. The base row of triangles will equal half the number of total triangles, rounded up to the next whole number. (Example: You'd like 9 triangles in your design. 9 divided by 2 is 4½. Round 4½ to 5 to equal the number of triangles in the base row.)

**Determine width of each triangle:** Divide your base row number into the width of your mounting board to determine how wide each finished triangle will be. (Example: You have 5 triangles on your base row and a 75"W mounting board. 75 divided by 5 = 15. Triangles will be 15"W at the point where they overhang the edge of the mounting board.)

**Determine length of each triangle:** The average length of a triangle valance is 18" from the top of the mounting board to the point. However, this measurement can be modified to fit the scale of your project.

**Make the triangle pattern:** On a large piece of paper, draw out a triangle to match the determined width measurement and 1½" taller than the height measurement. (The extra height will be used for mounting.) Draw a ½" seam allowance along each side edge of the triangle. Cut out the pattern.

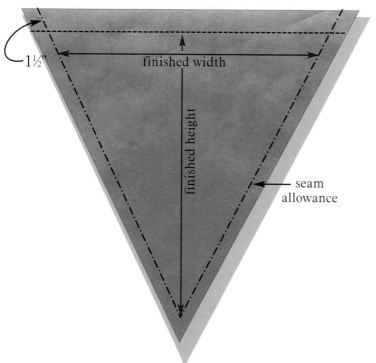

**Make the triangles:** Use the pattern to cut out the desired number of triangles from fabric. Cut out the same number of linings. If desired, sew cording to side edges of triangles. Sew fabric and linings together along side edges. Turn and press. Finishing the top edge of the triangle is unnecessary.

**Mount the base row:** Center one triangle on the mounting board with the top edge of the triangle overlapping the front edge of the mounting board 1½"; staple in place. Arrange

the remainder of the base row on the mounting board, adjusting the overlap of the triangles as needed. Leave about an inch of triangle overhanging each short end of the mounting board. Staple the remaining base row triangles in place, stapling the overhanging ends over the ends of the mounting board.

**Mount the top row:** Arrange the remaining triangles on top of the base row, making sure the points are centered between the openings created in the base row. Staple the triangles in place.

**Finish up:** Mount the board at the window with L-brackets.

# The No-Sew Valance

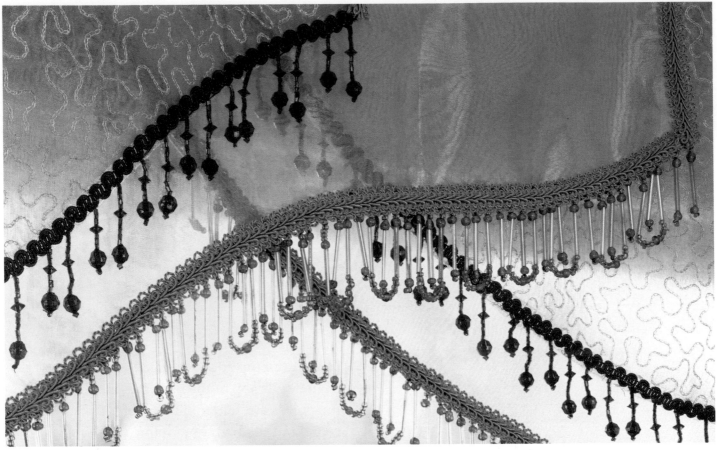

Who says you have to be able to sew to make a beautiful window treatment? We don't. Because you're not doing any complicated sewing, this is the perfect opportunity to make a lovely shaped bottom edge for the valance. You'll be glad you did.

## The Valance

**See an example:** A no-sew valance is shown on page 71.

**Gather your supplies:** You need a piece of 1x lumber (you can use 1x2, 1x4, or 1x6 lumber, depending on how far you wish your valance to extend away from the window), fabric, trims for the edge of the valance, double-sided adhesive tape, and L-brackets.

**Make the mounting board:** Measure the width of the window, including the frame; add at least 2" to allow L-brackets to be mounted. Cut your lumber to the measurement.

**Make the pattern:** Determine which edge is the front edge of the mounting board. Measure the front edge, left side edge, and right side edge. Add numbers together to determine the width of fabric to cut. Determine the longest finished point of your valance (18" is average; you may need to adjust); add 1½". Cut a piece of paper these measurements. Fold your paper in half to determine where the center point of the valance will be. Draw the desired shape from the fold to the outside edge and cut out through both layers to complete the pattern.

**Cut the fabric:** Use the pattern to cut out the valance from fabric.

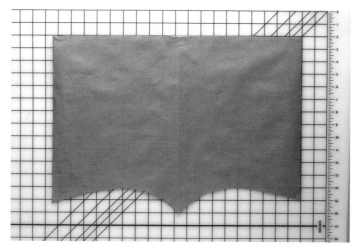

**Add the trim:** Working in small increments, used the double-sided tape to apply the trims to the side and bottom edges of the valance.

**Mount the valance on the board:** Center the valance on the mounting board with the top edge of the fabric overlapping the top of the board 1½"; staple in place. Fold the side edges to the side edges of the board, folding and stapling excess to top of the mounting board.

**Finish up:** Mount the board at the window using L-brackets.

# The Overlay

A simple overlay added to your no-sew valance takes your window treatment to new heights! Using a sheer fabric for the overlay is an elegant option.

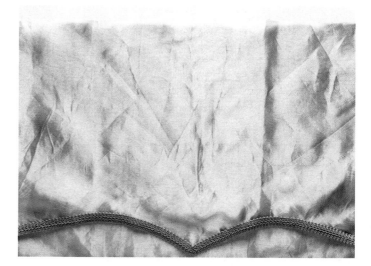

**How to proceed:** Cut the overlay fabric shorter than the length of the original valance – the amount shorter will depend on your design (We often use a piece 2"-3" shorter than the original). Finish the edges of the overlay as desired—cording is nice, a flashy trim or fringe may work well, or maybe they just need a simple hem. If your overlay fabric is lightweight and you're not going for the sheer look, you may need to line the overlay.

**Finish up:** Arrange overlay on top of the valance and secure with staples.

# The Dog-Ear Valance

We know this sounds like a crazy name, but the finished treatment is so cute! Basically, you make a plain valance— shirring tape gathers the top edge—and mount it on a mounting board. Ties shaped like a dog's floppy ears are tied around the valance, in effect shortening the valance and creating a scalloped bottom edge.

**Gather your supplies:** You need fabric for the valance and ties, small diameter cording, shirring tape, sewing supplies, a mounting board cut to the finished treatment width, stapler, and L-brackets.

**Prepare the valance:** Determine the finished length of your valance. Keep in mind that the ties will shorten your valance, so you may want it to be on the long side. Cut a valance 8" longer than the finished length and 2½ times wider than the finished width. Make a 2"W double hem on the bottom and top edges of the fabric. Make 1"W double hems on the side edges.

**Add the shirring tape:** Cut a piece of shirring tape 1" shorter than the current width of the valance. Center the shirring tape on the wrong side of the fabric 2" from the top edge. (The tape will start and stop ½" from the side edges of the valance). Stitch the tape in place through each of the channels in the tape (top and bottom edges and between each cord.) Knot cords at one end of tape. Pull cords from other end of tape until the top edge of the valance equals the length of the mounting board plus the side edges of the board. Knot cords and trim excess.

**Mount the valance:** Staple the valance to the mounting board through the shirring tape, aligning the top edge of the shirring tape with the top edge of the mounting board. Adjust the gathers as needed to hide the staples.

**Make the dog-ear tie pattern:** Determine how long the ties will need to be by tying scraps of fabric around the valance until you are happy with the length of fabric needed to tie up the valance to the right length. Make a pattern by drawing a 4"W rectangle that is half the finished length of your tie. Fold in half lengthwise. On one end of the pattern, widen the rectangle to resemble a dog-ear shape. Add a ½" seam allowance to the side and bottom edges. Cut out the pattern through both layers, then unfold. This pattern is ½ the length of the finished tie.

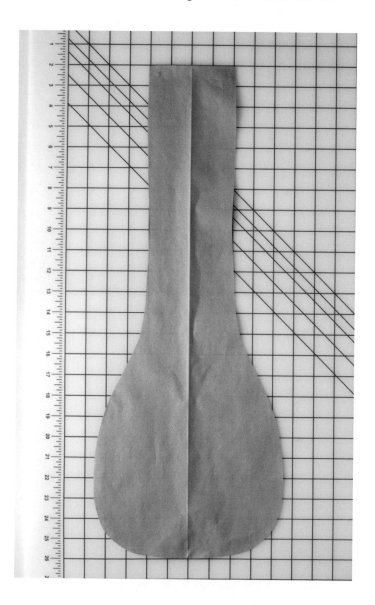

**Cut the ties:** Fold your tie fabric in half. Place the straight, short end of the pattern on the fold of the fabric and cut the tie. You'll need to cut two pieces for each tie.

**Complete the ties:** Sew cording to right side of one tie. Place a second tie on top and sew the two pieces together, leaving an opening along a straight edge for turning. Turn tie, slipstitch opening closed, and press. Make the remaining ties in the same way.

**Finish the job:** Drape the ties over the mounting board of the valance, spacing them to their approximate finished position. Use L-brackets to mount the treatment at the window, making sure that you will be able to slide the ties as needed to adjust. Tie the ties to the right height, and adjust the spacing and knot placement. You're done!

# The Reed Fencing Shade

This very custom shade is very easy to make and it's very inexpensive, too! The shade is made of reed fencing you buy at the home improvement store or nursery. The fencing usually comes in 6' x 15' rolls.

Basically, you'll be cutting a single piece of fencing that fits your finished width, but is long enough to drape over the mounting board to form a valance. Our example here shows an outside mount shade, using a 1x6 mounting board. Other sizes of mounting board could be used. An inside mounted shade also works well.

**Gather your supplies:** You need a 6' x 15' roll of reed fencing, 1x lumber in the desired width for the mounting board; L-brackets; wire cutters; utility knife; staple gun; 2 shade pulleys and a shade lock (available at fabric or drapery supply stores).

**Make the plan:** Determine how wide your finished shade will be. Also, determine how long the finished shade will be, how long the valance at the top will be, and how wide the mounting board is. Add these three numbers together to get the combined cut length of the shade.

**Cut the reed shade:** *Cut the correct width* – Cut reed to the desired finished width. You can cut the reeds with utility or old scissors. Try to cut the reed so that the wires that hold the fencing together will be centered.

*Cut the correct length* – Cut the fencing about 6" longer than the combined finished length. Untwist the wires and remove reeds at the top and bottom edges to obtain the correct length. Re-twist the wires together to secure and trim ends.

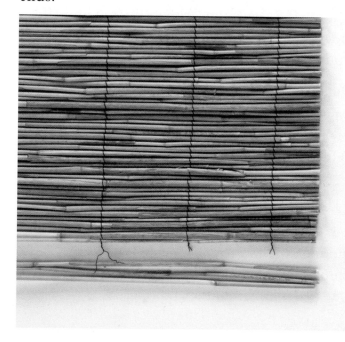

**Prepare the mounting board:** Cut the mounting board 4" shorter than the finished shade width. Cover the bottom of the mounting board by cutting reed to the same size and stapling it in place.

**Complete the shade:** Arrange the reed shade on the mounting board, so that the correct length for the valance goes over the front edge of the mounting board, and the remainder of the shade length falls over the back edge of the board. Making sure the shade is centered widthwise, staple in place on top of the mounting board. Follow the manufacturer's instructions to attach the pulley hardware and locking mechanism to the bottom of the mounting board.

**Mount the shade:** Use L-brackets to mount the shade at the window, cutting small holes in the reed, if needed, to accommodate the brackets.

# The Covered Rod

What could be better than making your own designer curtain rod that costs less than a pizza? Using rigid PVC pipe, also known as plastic plumbing pipe, is the secret.

## The Fabric-Covered Rod

**Gather your supplies:** Find the diameter of PVC pipe you'd like to use at your local home improvement or plumbing supply store. The larger diameter pipes are usually more rigid and will support your drapery better. Have it cut to the desired length (the helpful folks at the home store will do that for you). You will also need permanent spray adhesive, 100-grit sandpaper, fabric, and a permanent marker.

**Prepare your "rod":** Lightly sand the entire pipe, including the ends. Draw a straight line down the pipe from one end to the other.

**Prepare your fabric:** Cut a piece of fabric (pieced if needed) 6" longer than the pipe and 3" wider than the pipe's circumference (measure around the pipe). Press one long edge of the fabric 1½" to the wrong side. Open up the pressed area, spray lightly with adhesive and refold along the crease.

**Cover the rod:** Lightly spray the wrong side of the fabric piece with adhesive. With fabric centered, align the raw edge of the fabric along the drawn line on the rod and press in place.

Smooth the fabric around the rod. You may need extra adhesive where the fabric edges overlap.

**Finish up:** Lightly spray the inside of the cut pipe ends with adhesive. Tuck excess fabric into rod. Attach finials to the ends of the rod.

## The Fabric-Shirred Rod

Shirred (gathered) fabric can cover up a variety of sins, including an inexpensive or just plain ugly rod. See page 77 for an example.

**Gather your supplies:** You need the rod you'll be covering, fabric, sewing supplies, and spray adhesive.

**Cut your fabric:** Cut a piece of fabric (pieced if needed) 3 times longer than the rod and 1½" wider than the rod's circumference (measure around the rod).

**Make the fabric tube:** Fold fabric in half lengthwise, right sides together. Use a ½" seam to sew the long edges of the fabric together. Turn right side out.

**Finish up:** Insert rod into the fabric tube, distributing the gathers of fabric evenly. To finish, spray the inside of the rod with adhesive and tuck the fabric ends inside the rod, or simply tuck the fabric ends inside the fabric tube and whipstitch the ends closed.

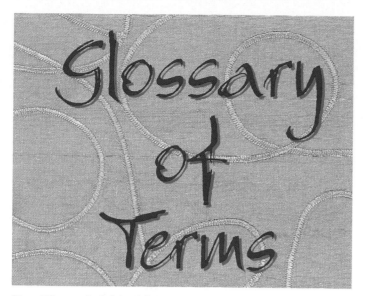

## Glossary of Terms

**Box Pleat:** A fold of fabric spaced evenly apart to add fullness.

**Bullion Fringe:** Woven twisted yarns of thread that form a thick fringe.

**Casing:** A fold of fabric, which makes a pocket after stitching, in which a rod may pass through.

**Center Draw:** A single pair of draperies that open and close at the center of a window.

**Center Support:** A bracket placed at the center of a window to prevent a rod from sagging.

**Cornice:** A decorative box-like accessory usually made of wood and upholstered in fabric or covered in another manner.

**Cut Length (or Width):** Length (or width) of fabric after all allowances (hems, header, etc.) have been added.

**Draw Drapes:** Panels of fabric that are retractable.

**Facing:** A piece of fabric used to conceal raw edges or to produce a stronger finish; it also may be used in a decorative fashion.

**Finials:** The decorative embellishment placed at the end of a rod.

**Finished Length (or Width):** The length (or width) of a completed project.

**Gimp:** A flat braid used to trim drapes or upholstery.

**Heading:** Top part of the drapery that accommodates the pleats, usually 2"-3" high.

**Hem:** The finished edge of a sewn piece of fabric usually turned up and stitched and referred to as the bottom of the drapery.

**Holdbacks:** A decorative piece of hardware placed on either side of a window specifically to hold draperies to the side.

**Interlining:** A thick felt-like fabric used between the main fabric and the lining to enhance insulation value and protect fabrics from fading. It also adds weight to the drapery for a more substantial look.

**Jabot:** A decorative fabric cascade, often used in pairs, that enhances swags.

**Lining:** Fabric that is placed to the back of decorative fabric to protect, insulate, and enhance the way the drapery hangs.

**Mounting Board:** Usually 1x4, 1x6, or 1x8 lumber upon which valances, swags, balloons, etc. are built. The board is then mounted to the wall with brackets.

**One-Way Draw:** Draperies designed to open one way only.

**Panel:** A straight drop of drapery.

**Projection:** The measurement to which the drapery rod extends out from the wall.

**Puddle:** A term used to describe the way a drapery is sometimes made longer that the measured distance from rod to floor to suggest luxuriousness.

**Rod Pocket:** A hollow opening at the top or bottom of a panel or valance in which a rod is inserted.

**Sash:** Sheer fabric gathered and fastened close to the window by a sash rod.

**Swag:** A piece of fabric gathered or pleated on the sides so that the center hangs in a curve.

**Tassel Fringe:** A decorative tassel trim bound together by a decorative gimp.

**Valance:** A horizontal top section of a treatment, usually made of fabric, used mainly for decorative purposes or to conceal drapery hardware.

**Width:** A piece of fabric measured from selvage to selvage. It may take several widths of fabric to make a drapery.

To our clients and homeowners, who invited us into their homes and lives to design beautiful windows and to take photos, we extend our grateful thanks.

Brent and Stacy Begin
Paul and Tracie Benson
Dan and Cy Bowers
Mary Jane Bowers
Pam Bryant
Perry and Mary Campbell
Chris and Amy Carper
Shirley A. Clingmon
Pat Crews
Kim and Judy Davis
Bill and Debby Denton
Billy and Winona Glaze
Dwight and Suzanne Harned
Gary and Trisha Holt
Craig and Alisa Johnson
Kim and Peggy Mooney
Linda Newman
Mr. and Mrs. E. A. Ostedgaard
Tyler and Tracy Pate
Dr. and Mrs. Paul C. Peek
Stephen Pickering
Bruce and September Rew
Gary and Becky Rickenbach
Dan and Cheri Rolett
Chris and Lori Schaffhauser
Rob and Luanne Seay
Tom and Kellie Shirley
Scarlett Smith
Ralph and Karen Strack
Andrea Tomlinson
Sissie Turner

We'd like to thank these businesses who graciously contributed to our book: Curtains Etc.; Cynthia East Fabrics; David Claiborne, LTD; Denise Simons Interiors; Fabulous Finds Antique and Decorative Malls; Ina's Window Fashions; Larry's, Inc.; Linda's Window Decor and More; Lisa's Closet; Pier One, North Little Rock, Arkansas; Rye Fine Furniture and Interiors; Sew Creative Windows; Simons Interiors; Southern Wholesale Florist; Three-D-Design; Window Expressions; and Young@Art.

Thanks also to Mark Mathews of The Peerless Group, Little Rock, Arkansas, for capturing the beauty of each window through his lens, and to Amy Carper of Carper Creative Photography for making us feel relaxed in front of her lens. A special thanks to Sandra Case, Alisa Johnson, and Amy King—we couldn't have done this book without you.

Finally, we lovingly acknowledge the most important people in our lives: our husbands, Marco Brolo and Kevin Charton, and also our families. Their love and support of us in all our endeavors is priceless.